Shape

by
Karen Bryant-Mole

**Illustrated by
John Yates**

Notes for teachers and parents

This book introduces children to 2D and 3D shapes. It looks at angles, nets, symmetry and the movement of shapes.

Understanding Maths

Adding and Subtracting
Numbers
Measurement
Shape
Graphs and Charts
Multiplying and Dividing

Series editor Deborah Elliott
Edited by Zoë Hargreaves
Designed by Ross George
Commissioned photography by Zul Mukhida

First published in 1991 by
Wayland (Publishers) Limited
61 Western Road, Hove,
East Sussex BN3 1JD

British Library Cataloguing in Publication Data
Bryant-Mole, Karen
Shape. - (Understanding Maths)
I. Title II. Series
372.7
ISBN 0 7502 0016 2

Phototypeset by Ross George
Printed by G. Canale and C.S.p.A., Turin
Bound by Casterman S.A., Belgium

Contents

Triangles, circles, rectangles and squares

This road sign is shaped like a triangle. It has three straight sides and three corners. It is a rather unusual sign. It means ' Watch out for toads!'

Below are three more signs. One is shaped like a circle, one like a rectangle and the other like a square.

A circle is perfectly round.

A rectangle has four sides with opposite sides the same length.

A square has four sides which are all the same length.

Look at the signs below and decide which sign is which shape.

The proper name for the corner of a shape is the 'vertex'. The word for more than one vertex is 'vertices'. Match up each description opposite with one of the shapes.

All circles look very similar. The only thing that can change is the size. Squares also look quite similar, although sometimes they can be more difficult to recognize when they are tipped up on one vertex.

  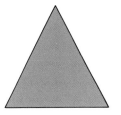 

a) Three sides and three vertices
b) Four sides the same length and four vertices
c) One side and no vertices
d) Four sides with opposite sides the same length and
   four vertices.

Rectangles can look very different from one another. One might be tall and narrow and another short and wide.

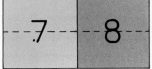

Look at this shape. Within it are nine rectangles.

Here they all are:

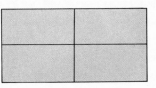 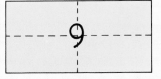

Triangles can also look very different from one another.
Look at this shape.
Can you find thirteen triangles?

Make up your own puzzle like this using squares.

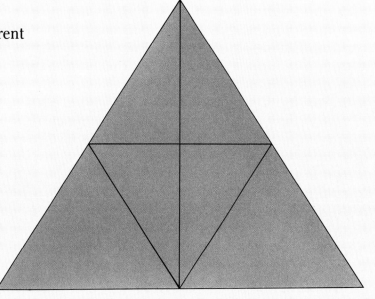

Quadrilaterals

This kite has four straight sides. Any shape with four straight sides is called a quadrilateral.

All of these shapes are quadrilaterals.

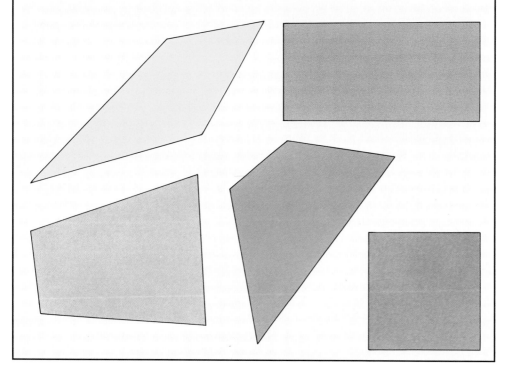

Rectangles are special types of quadrilaterals.
A rectangle must have four square corners or right angles.
A square is even more special. It is a rectangle with all four sides the same length.

Make your own right angle

Cut out a circle of paper. Fold the circle in half and then fold it in half again. The square corner you have made is a right angle.

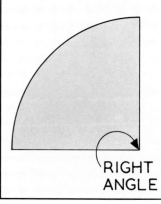

RIGHT ANGLE

These kites are all quadrilaterals because they all have four straight sides.

Two are also rectangles, because they have four square corners or right angles.

One is a square, because it not only has four right angles but also has four sides the same length.

Look at each kite and decide whether you would describe it as 'quadrilateral', 'rectangle' or 'square'. Use the square corner you made from the circle of paper to help you.

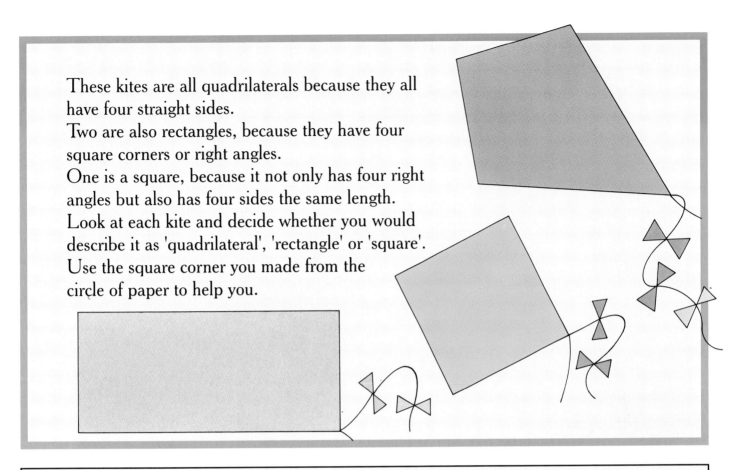

Make a quadrilateral jigsaw puzzle

You will need an old birthday or Christmas card. Cut off the back of the card so only the picture remains. Turn the picture over and, with a pen, start to divide the card up into four-sided shapes. It is easiest to start in one corner and work your way across the rest of the card. When the card is finished, cut out all the quadrilaterals.

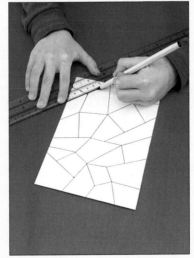

Turn the pieces over and see how long it takes you to do the puzzle.

Parallelograms

Right angles are very important when building a house. The doorways and windows have to be made very accurately. Nobody wants a house with sloping doors or windows!

Rhombus

There is also another special type of parallelogram, which has four sides the same length.
If it had four right angles it would be a square. If it doesn't it is called a rhombus. A rhombus is the same shape as a diamond in a pack of cards.

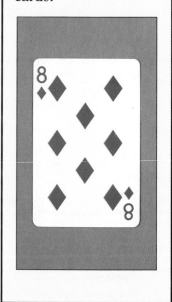

The doorway has two long sides. They are exactly the same distance apart at the top of the doorway as they are at the bottom. No matter how long you made those sides they would never meet. Opposite lines that never meet are called parallel lines.

A quadrilateral in which both pairs of opposite sides are parallel is called a parallelogram.

The doorway and window both make parallelograms.

As well as being parallel, the opposite sides of a parallelogram are always the same length.

All rectangles are a type of parallelogram. It is impossible to make a shape with four right angles and opposite sides the same length that does not have parallel sides.

Look at each of these shapes. They are all quadrilaterals. Most of them are also parallelograms. Some of them can also be described as rectangles and you might find a square or a rhombus.

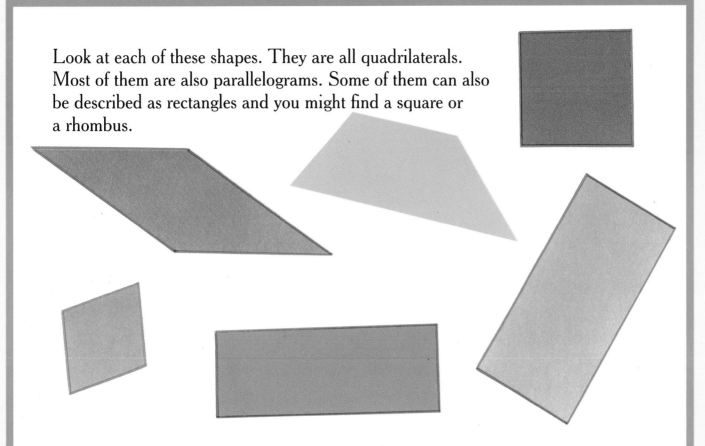

Use the questions and answers in this chart to work out the most precise description of each of the shapes above.

To help you, sides that are the same length have been drawn in the same colour.

Remember, right angles are square corners and parallel lines are lines that would never join up no matter how long you made them.

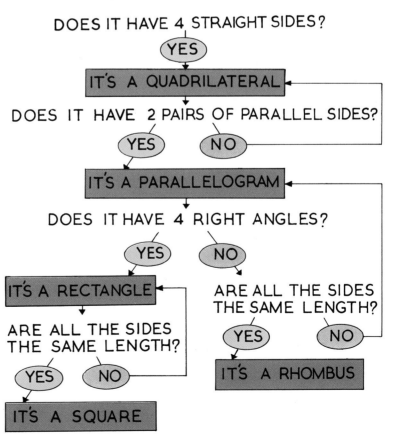

DOES IT HAVE 4 STRAIGHT SIDES?
YES
IT'S A QUADRILATERAL
DOES IT HAVE 2 PAIRS OF PARALLEL SIDES?
YES   NO
IT'S A PARALLELOGRAM
DOES IT HAVE 4 RIGHT ANGLES?
YES   NO
IT'S A RECTANGLE   ARE ALL THE SIDES THE SAME LENGTH?
ARE ALL THE SIDES THE SAME LENGTH?   YES   NO
YES   NO
IT'S A RHOMBUS
IT'S A SQUARE

Polygons

Shapes with many sides are called polygons.
Polygons have special names depending on how many sides they have.
Each piece of chocolate in this bar has six sides. A shape with six sides is a hexagon.
A five-sided shape is a pentagon.

Look at the soccer ball below.
You will see that the pattern on it is made up of pentagons and hexagons.
What are the red shapes called?

Look carefully at one of the red pentagons.

Each side is the same length and the angle or shape of each corner is the same too.

Polygons with sides that are all the same length and angles that are the same are called regular polygons.
The red shapes on the ball are regular pentagons and the white shapes are regular hexagons.

There is an easy way to tell if a shape is a regular polygon or not.
Turn the shape round so that each flat edge in turn is towards you.
If the shape looks the same, no matter which edge is towards you, it is a regular polygon.

A shape with eight sides is called an octagon. This is easy to remember because an octopus has eight legs.

Making a regular octagon

Cut a piece of paper into a circle by drawing around something circular, such as the rim of a bowl, and cutting it out. Fold the circle in half then in half again. You should have a piece that looks like a quarter of a cake. Fold it in half once more. With a ruler, draw a straight line from the end of one side to the other. Cut along that line. Open it out to find your octagon.

Here is a stained glass window. It looks beautiful when the sunlight shines through the coloured glass.

Make a stained glass window

Cut out a large regular octagon from a sheet of black paper. Draw lots of polygons on the paper (they don't have to be regular polygons). Cut them out. Glue different coloured pieces of tissue paper on to the paper to cover the holes. Turn it over and hang it in front of a window.

Tessellation

If you look carefully at the netting on this rabbit hutch you will see that it is made up of lots of hexagons.

Hexagons can be arranged so that they make a pattern with no spaces.

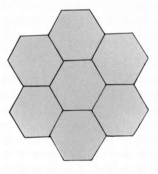

A pattern with no gaps between the shapes is called a tessellation.

Try your own tessellations

Cut out some pages from an old magazine. Fold each page in half lengthwise and cut down the fold line to give yourself a number of rectangular pieces of paper. Try to arrange the pieces in the designs shown on the left and then see if you can find a different way to tessellate your rectangles.

Rectangles make very good tessellations. Here are two ways to arrange rectangles into a tessellation.

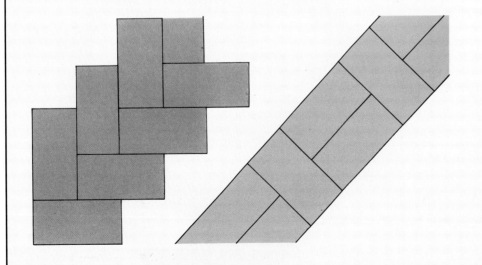

Here are some more tiling patterns. Look at them and decide which of these shapes tessellate; circle, triangle, regular pentagon.

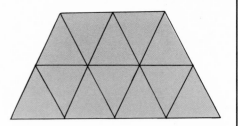

You can make tiling patterns using a mixture of shapes. Which shapes have been used to make this pathway?

A tessellation bookmark

Make some small templates by tracing the shapes below on to card and cutting them out. Use a ruler when you are tracing to make sure your lines are straight.

Draw around your templates on bright coloured paper. Cut out lots of each shape. Cut a piece of card into a rectangle that is 5 cm wide and 20 cm

long. Design your tessellation by covering the card with your cut-out pieces. Glue down the pieces when you are happy with your design.

Angles

The minute hand of the clock in the picture above is pointing straight up. The hour hand is pointing out to the side. It is 3 o'clock.

The picture on the right shows the clock 5 minutes later. It is 5 minutes past 3 o'clock. The minute hand has moved nearer the hour hand.
Both hands on the clock move in the same direction, from 1 to 2 and 2 to 3 and so on. The direction the hands move around the clock is called clockwise. The opposite of clockwise is anticlockwise. If the hands of the clock went backwards from 12 to 11 and 11 to 10 etc, it would be anticlockwise movement.

If you look at the minute hand and the hour hand of the clock you will see that they form an angle or corner at the centre of the clock.

At 3 o'clock the angle formed by the two hands is a right angle.

At 5 minutes past 3 the angle is much smaller. An angle that is smaller than a right angle is called an acute angle.

Play 'Duck, Duck, Goose'

Ask some friends to sit in a circle. You will be the caller. Walk around the outside of the circle in a clockwise

The time on the left shows it is just after half past 10. Look at the minute hand. (It's always the longer hand.) Now look at the hour hand. The angle formed between the minute hand and the hour hand, looking in a clockwise direction, is much bigger than a right angle.
An angle that is bigger than a right angle is called an obtuse angle.

See if you can work out whether each of these clocks shows an acute, obtuse or right angle. Always look at the minute hand first and then look towards the hour hand in a clockwise direction.

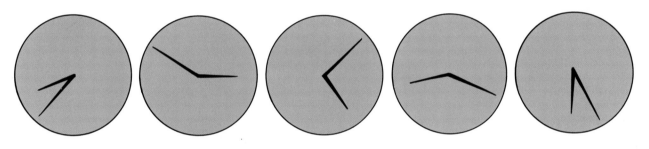

direction saying 'duck' to each friend in turn and tapping the friend on the head. Then instead of saying 'duck', you say 'goose' to one of the players. That player has to run around the circle in an anticlockwise direction while you run in a clockwise direction. The first person back to the space in the circle sits down. The person still standing is the caller.

3D shapes

All the shapes we have met so far have been 2D or two dimensional shapes. 2D shapes are flat shapes. You can measure how tall and wide they are but not how thick they are. In this picture Paul is working at his desk.

Look carefully at the grey box in front of him. As well as measuring its height from the bottom to the top and its width from side to side, you could also measure its depth (or thickness) from back to front. Shapes like these are called 3D or three dimensional shapes and they have a different set of names to the 2D shapes.

The box in the picture has six flat surfaces or faces. All of the faces are shaped like rectangles. A 3D shape with rectangular faces is called a cuboid.

Paul's notepad also has six faces but each of these faces is the same size. All of the faces are shaped like squares.

A 3D shape with six square faces is called a cube. Next to the notepad is a stick of glue.

It has a flat face at either end shaped like a circle and a curved surface. Shapes like these are called cylinders.

At the end of the table is a round globe which shows the different countries of the world. If Paul spins the globe round it will look the same shape no matter which way he looks at it. Shapes like these are called spheres. Spheres have no flat surfaces.

Each of the flat surfaces of these shapes is called a face. The line made where two faces join is called the edge. The corners where the edges join are called vertices (just like the corners of a 2D shape).
Which shapes have twelve edges?
Which shapes have eight vertices?
Which shape has two faces?
Which shape has no faces?

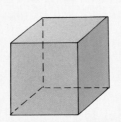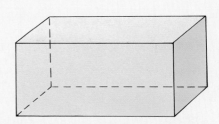

What shapes do these objects remind you of?

Shape quiz

See if you can make up some quiz questions to ask a friend.
Here are some to start you off;

1. I am thinking of a sphere that you might use with two racquets and a net.
2. I am thinking of a cube that is used in games like snakes and ladders.
3. I am thinking of a cylinder that you might buy soup in.
4. I am thinking of a cuboid that is used to build walls.

Answers
1. a tennis ball 2. a dice 3. a tin 4. a brick

17

Pyramids and prisms

Here are some tents. The tent at the front is shaped like a pyramid. The tents behind are rather like prisms.

Pyramids and prisms are two groups of 3D shapes.

All prisms have two ends the same shape and sides that are parallelograms.

All of these shapes are prisms.

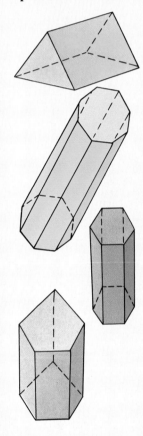

Look at these churches. One shows a prism, one shows a cone and one shows a pyramid.

Which is which?

All pyramids have a flat face at the bottom with three or more edges and triangles for all the other faces.
The triangular faces slope up to meet at a point.

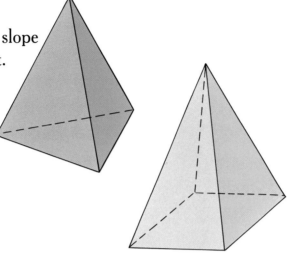

Pyramids have different names according to the shape of the face at the bottom.
A pyramid with a triangle at the bottom is a triangular pyramid. One with a square is a square pyramid. A five-sided base makes a pentagonal pyramid and a six-sided base makes a hexagonal pyramid. Look at the pyramids again and find one of each type.

Prisms have different names according to the shape of the ends. A prism with triangular ends is a triangular prism, and so on. Look at the prisms again and try to identify a triangular prism, a pentagonal prism, a hexagonal prism and an octagonal prism.

Helene's wizard's hat has a shape rather like a cone.
A cone has a face at the bottom shaped like a circle and a curved surface which slopes up to a point.

19

Nets

Jane is making a kitchen cupboard. The cupboard is a self-assembly unit. That means that you buy all the pieces needed for the cupboard and then you make it yourself.

Here are the pieces needed to make the cupboard.

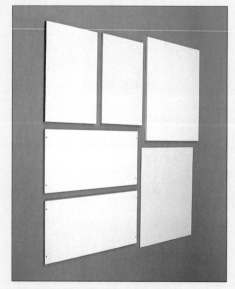

This is what it looks like when it is finished.

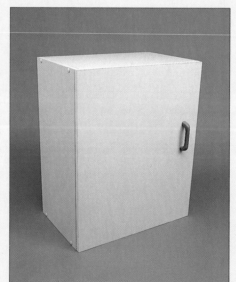

The finished cupboard is shaped like a cuboid.
Six rectangles are needed to make this cuboid.
If it had been made from six squares would the finished cupboard be a square pyramid or a cube?

Here is a triangular prism.

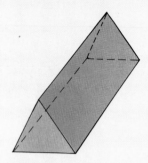

Which of the groups of 2D shapes below makes this prism?

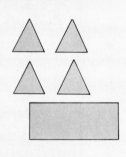

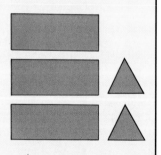

20

The cupboard was put together using six separate rectangles, but it is possible to make 3D shapes by folding one 2D shape.

If you were to cut out this shape and fold it along the dotted lines you would make a cube.
A 2D shape that can be folded to make a 3D shape is called a net.

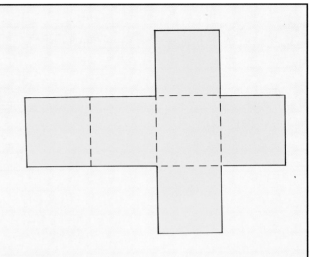

Make your own cube

Find a cube-shaped building brick. Place it on a piece of thin card and draw around the base. Lift the brick and place it next to the square you have already drawn. Draw around the base again. Carry on until you have a shape that looks like the one above.

Cut it out and fold it into a cube. Secure the edges with sticky tape.

A cube has more than one net. Here is a different net. Try making this one too.

Devise another net that can be made up into a cube?

There are eleven possible nets altogether.

Make a net of a cuboid

Find a cuboid-shaped box. Place the box on a large piece of card. Draw around the base of the box and then slowly roll the box over on to the next side. Make sure the edge of the box is in line with the side you have already drawn and then draw around the box again. Roll the box twice more, making sure it is in the correct position. Add the ends of the box by putting the box back on the first rectangle and standing it first to one side and then to the other, drawing around each end. Cut it out and fold it into a cuboid. Secure the edges with sticky tape. Why not decorate your box.

Symmetry

This butterfly is an example of symmetry. A shape is symmetrical when both sides match up exactly. The butterfly's body forms a line down the middle which is called the line of symmetry or the axis of symmetry.

Find a small mirror with straight sides and look at these shapes.

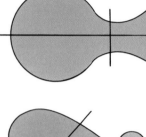

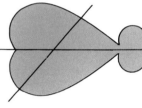

Each shape has two lines drawn in. Only one is the line of symmetry. Put your mirror along each line and look at the reflection.

Find the line of symmetry

Trace this shape. Cut it out and fold it in half so that one half fits exactly on top of the other half. Open it out again. The fold line is the line of symmetry.

This type of symmetry is called reflective symmetry because one half looks like a mirror reflection of the other half. It can also be called bi-lateral or flip symmetry.

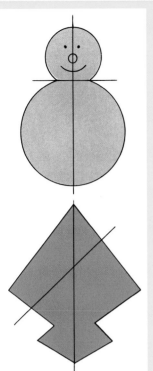

If the shape you see is the same as the shape without the mirror, then that is the line of symmetry. Find the correct line of symmetry for each shape.

Some shapes have more than one line of symmetry. Place your mirror along each of the lines on this triangle shape. Each time you will see the same shape as you would without the mirror.

This shape has two lines of symmetry. Can you find them both?

Another type of symmetry is rotational symmetry. A shape has rotational symmetry if it can be turned and fitted exactly on to its outline more than once in a complete turn. Trace the square below. Use a coloured crayon to draw the top line. If you turn your tracing round you will find that it can fit on top of the original shape four times before the coloured line is back at the top.

The number of times a shape can fit on top of itself is called the order of symmetry. A square has rotational symmetry of order four.

What order of rotational symmetry do these shapes have?

Trace these shapes and remember to mark one of the lines with a coloured crayon.

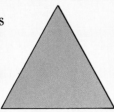
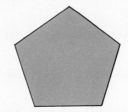
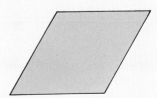

Reflection and translation

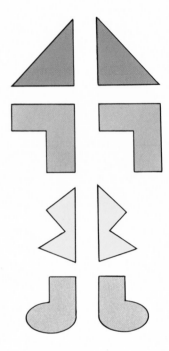

In this photograph you can see two views of a monument in India called the Taj Mahal. The picture you can see in the water is an image of the top picture. Images that show the same shapes flipped over are called reflections.

Above are some pairs of shapes. Most of them are examples of reflections but one is not. Which pair is the odd one out?

Make an image showing reflection

Find a large piece of paper and fold it in half. Unfold it and paint a picture on one half only. Fold the paper in half again and gently rub all over the paper.
Open the paper to see your picture reflected on to the other half of the paper.

Translation

Shapes can move in other ways too.
These images do not show reflection because the shape has not been flipped over. Instead the images have been made by moving the shapes up, down and sideways.
This sliding movement is called translation.

Look at these pairs of shapes.
Most show translation but one does not.
Which one is it?

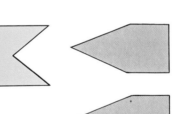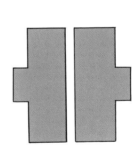

Potato translation!

You can make images which show translation using a potato! Cut a potato in half and then cut away the edges to leave a shape in the middle. Hold the uncut end of the potato and dip the cut end into some paint. Make a print of your shape on a piece of paper. Continue to make prints all over the page, holding the potato in the same position without twisting your hand. All the prints will be translations of the original print.

Rotation

The blades on this helicopter go round in a turning movement. When a shape is turned to make another image the movement is called rotation. The helicopter blades turn round a point in the middle. This point is called the centre of rotation or the turn centre.

Making rotation images

Trace this shape on to a piece of card, remembering the black dot. Cut out the shape and attach it to another piece of the card by putting a paper fastener through the black dot and the bottom piece of card.
Draw around the shape. Move the

Find out which of these pairs of shapes show rotation. With tracing paper, trace over the green shape and mark in the black dot. This will be your centre of rotation. Now turn your tracing paper round, keeping the black dot in the middle. If the tracing fits on to the orange shape exactly then the orange shape is a rotation of the green shape.

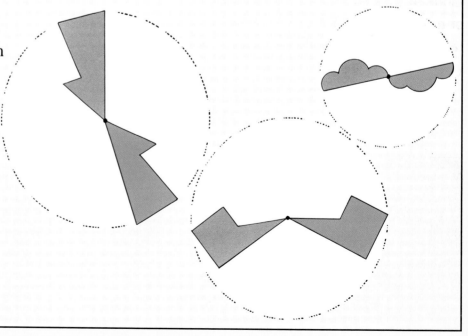

shape round and draw around it again. You can draw around the shape anywhere within the turn.

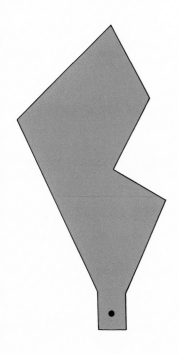

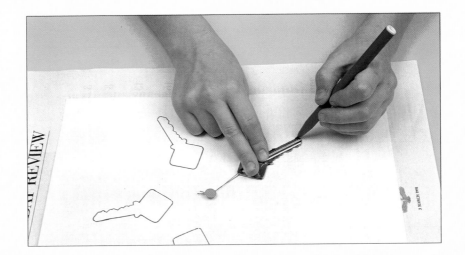

Cut a piece of cotton thread about 10 cm long. Thread it through the hole in a key and tie the ends. Place a piece of paper on top of a thick newspaper. Put a drawing pin through the loop of the thread attached to the key and pin the drawing pin to the paper and newspaper. Gently pull out the key so that the thread is pulled straight. Draw around the key. Keep the drawing pin in the same position while moving the key to another position in the circle. Any shape you draw will be a rotation of the first shape.

Look at these photographs and decide which type of movement you think each one shows. Is it reflection (a flip), translation (a slide) or rotation (a turn)?

Congruent shapes

Maggie is making a skirt. She is pinning the pattern pieces on to the material, ready for cutting out. Maggie needs to use one of the pieces twice. She knows that when she comes to cut out the second piece she can place the pattern anywhere on the material and the shape will be the same as the first one. She could even turn the pattern piece over! Shapes which are exactly alike but which are not necessarily in the same position are called congruent shapes.

Look at these pieces of material and decide whether the pattern was moved in a slide, or a flip when they were being cut out.

Congruent shapes are often found in wallpaper designs like these. Which shows translation? Which shows reflection? and which shows rotation?

Here are six triangles. There are three pairs of congruent triangles. Can you find them? Use tracing paper to trace one triangle. Now find out which of the other triangles you can fit your tracing on to exactly. (Remember, you can slide or turn your tracing paper. You can even flip it over!)

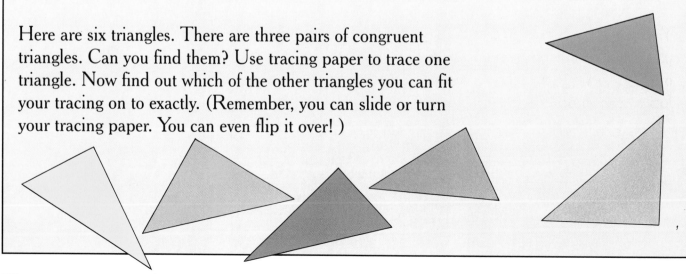

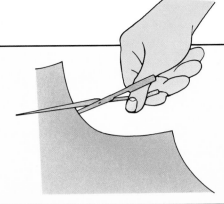

As you can see all the pieces are identical because they all fit on top of one another exactly. Congruent shapes will always fit directly on top of one another, although you may have to move them around a little at first.

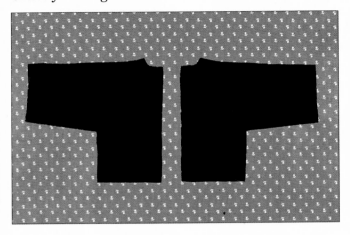

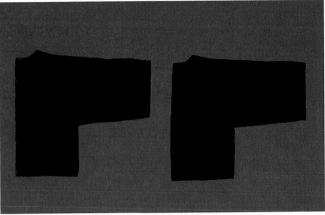

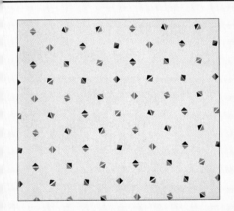

You can design your own birthday or Christmas wrapping paper. Draw a picture, such as a Christmas tree, on to a piece of card. Cut out the picture and use it as a template to draw lots of copies on to a trace.

Glossary

congruent	identical except for position
net	a flat shape that can be folded to make a 3D shape
parallelogram	a four-sided shape with opposite sides parallel
polygon	a closed shape with sides that are straight lines
prism	a 3D shape with ends the same shape and sides that are parallelograms
pyramid	a 3D shape with a flat surface at the bottom and triangles for all other faces
quadrilateral	a 2D shape with four sides
reflection	movement where the image is flipped over
rhombus	a quadrilateral with all four sides the same length
rotation	movement where the image is turned round a centre point
sphere	a 3D shape that is perfectly round, like a ball
tessellation	a tiling pattern with no gaps between the shapes
translation	movement where the image is slid

Books to read

Investigating Shapes, Ed Catherall (Wayland, 1983)
Rectangles, Graham Percy, (Blackie, 1984)
Squares, Graham Percy (Blackie, 1984)
Shapes, John Satchwell (Walker Books, 1988)

The photographs in this book were supplied by Chapel Studios.

The publisher wishes to thank all those individuals, particularly the children, who participated in and helped with the commissioned photography for this book, especially B & Q who provided the cupboard used on page 20.

Index